SCIENCE-*OLOGY*

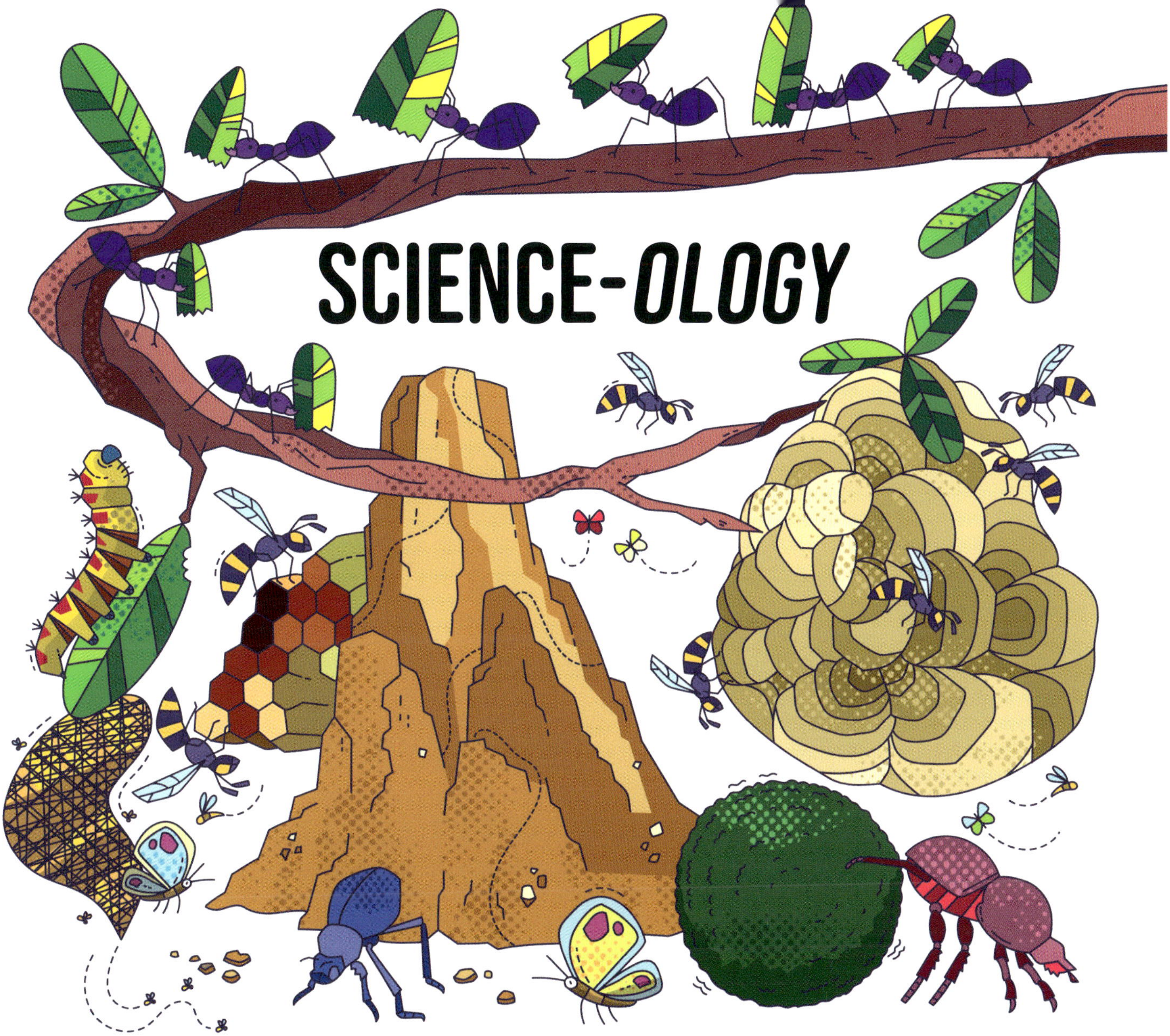

ENTOMOLOGY

ANNA CLAYBOURNE
DANIEL LIMÓN

I0806950

PowerKiDS press™

Published in 2026 by The Rosen Publishing Group, Inc.
2544 Clinton Street, Buffalo, NY 14224

First published in Great Britain in 2023 by Wayland
Copyright © Hodder and Stoughton, 2023

Editor: Elise Short
Consultant: Buglife, the Invertebrate Conservation Trust
Design: Rocket Design (East Anglia) Ltd
Illustrations: Daniel Limón

Cataloging-in-Publication Data

Names: Claybourne, Anna, author. | Limón, Daniel Sanchez, illustrator.

Title: Entomology / by Anna Claybourne, illustrated by Daniel Limón.

Description: Buffalo, NY : PowerKids Press, 2026. | Series: Science-ology | Includes glossary and index.

Identifiers: ISBN 9781499454697 (pbk.) | ISBN 9781499454703 (library bound) | ISBN 9781499454710 (ebook)

Subjects: LCSH: Entomology--Juvenile literature.

Classification: LCC QL467.2 C539 2026 | DDC 595.7--dc23

All rights reserved.

Picture credits: Alamy: Alister Doyle/Reuters 9b; Tim Gainey 45t.

© Dr Frank Glaw 18b.

Science Photo Library: Cecile Degremont/Look At Sciences 41b; Louise Murray 33t; Philippe Psaila 15c.

Shutterstock: Adopik 5br, 6cl; Akiyoko 28tr; Akor86 7bl; Alle 23b; Rashad Ashur 7br; Salvador Aznar 11tr; Bhupinder Bagga 38clb; Manuel Balesteri 24b; BNP Design Studio 15t; Henk Bogaard 32b; Sonboon Bunproy 41c; CL-Medien 27t; Cornel Constantin 16c; Creative icon styles 13bl; Jacky D 16t; Angel DiBilio 33b; Fire-n 31l; Freedomnaruk 32c; Petr Ganaj 37br; Japan's Fireworks 36t; Pavel Klimenko 45b; Krikkiat 8bl; Kungfu01 38cl; Tim Lamprey 25bl; Henrdik Larsson 20b; Russell Marshall 35b; Mentalmind 44t; Frances van der Merwe 22b; MyFavoriteTime 26c; N Style 5brc, 11tl; Nechaevkon 12t; New Africa 38tr; Nico99 24t; Oleg1824 4; Andrey Pavlov 40b; Phakamat BL 38cr; Ondrej Prosicky 30c; Protasov AN 15b, 30tl, 30tc,30bl, 30br, 39; Jeff Reeves 32t; Sue Robinson 19bl; Roncsakj 38tl; Rustic 34b;Sakurra 26cr; Serg64 8bg; Nippich Somsaard 31r; Sundry Photography 12b; Tavizta 5bl; TRR 28tl; Danut Vieru 30tr; Birute Vijeikiene 11b; Vladvm 6tl; WildlifeWorld 38crb; Wild Media 5tr; Tom Wurl 23t; Yanochka88 9t; Peter Yeeles 34t.

Wikimedia Commons;Cueva de la Arana, Spain 6bc; Geschenk von Louise Bachofen-Burckhardt 1904, Joseph Marrell 1679, 21b; Robert Hooke Micrographia 1665 7cr; Metamorphosis insectorum Surinamensium 1705 21t.

The website addresses (URLs) included in this book were valid at the time of going to press. However, it is possible that contents or addresses may have changed since the publication of this book. No responsibility for any such changes can be accepted by either the author or the Publisher.

Every attempt has been made to clear copyright. Should there be any inadvertent omission please apply to the publisher for rectification.

No part of this book may be reproduced in any form without permission in writing from the publisher, except by a reviewer.

Manufactured in the United States of America

CPSIA Compliance Information: Batch #CSPK26. For further information contact Rosen Publishing at 1-800-237-9932.

Find us on

CONTENTS

INSECTS ARE EVERYWHERE!

Bees buzzing by, ants under the ground, countless caterpillars, millions of midges ... insects may be small, but there are a LOT of them! The study of insects, or entomology, is fun and fascinating – and also very important.

Insects and humans

Insects have played a big part in our lives ever since humans first existed. They affect us in all kinds of ways – some helpful, some harmful.

They can spread diseases in their bites – or just give you a painful sting.

Insects are often beautiful, and have inspired art and design since ancient times.

They provide useful products, such as silk from silk moths and honey from honeybees.

They can be parasites, such as head lice and fleas, that live and feed on us.

They can be pests, eating our crops and stored food.

While some insects eat our crops, other insects can help us by eating those insect pests!

Insects and the world

Insects aren't just important for humans, but for the whole natural world. Insect species make up a big part of the world's biodiversity, or range of different living things. They're a vital part of the food chain, as vast numbers of insects become food for birds, lizards, spiders, bats, fish, and many other creatures.

Some insects carry pollen from one flower to another as they feed, helping plants to make seeds. Others are decomposers and recyclers: they eat dead plants and animals, breaking them down into chemicals and returning them to the soil.

Birds called bee-eaters get their name because they love eating bees! As part of their courtship, the male gives the female tasty bees as gifts.

Is it an insect?

Take a look at this beetle to see the main insect body parts and features.

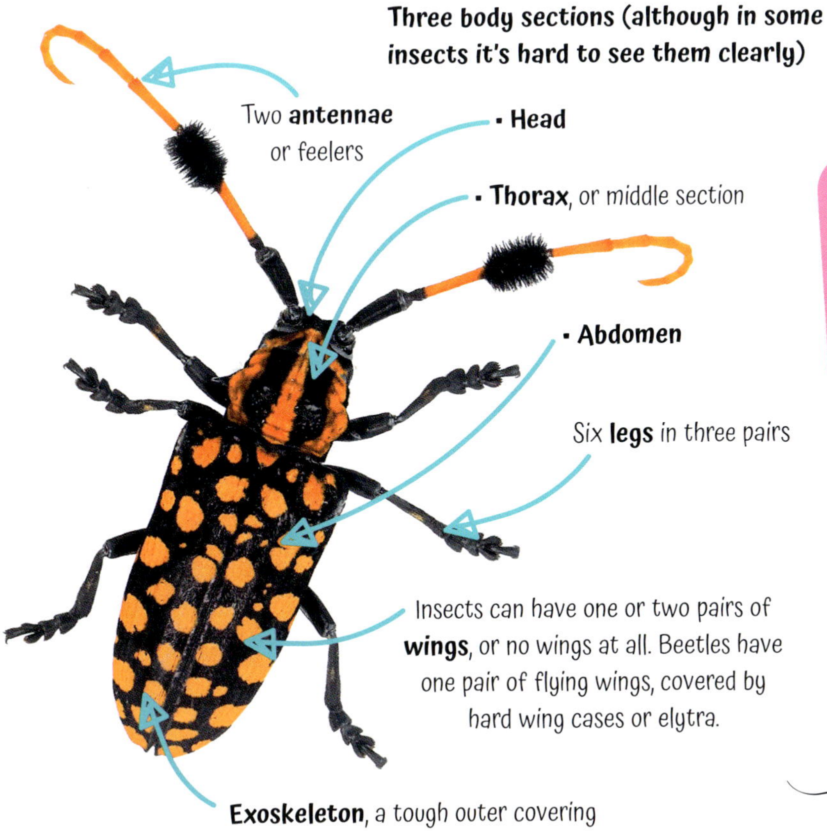

INSECTS IN NUMBERS

- We have discovered around 1 million different types, or species, of insects so far.
- One-third of them are beetles!
- At any one time, scientists estimate there are around 10 quintillion, or 10,000,000,000,000,000,000 insects on the planet.
- That's over 1.3 billion insects for each person on Earth!

THE SCIENCE OF ENTOMOLOGY

As there are SO many insects, entomology is a big, big topic, with many branches and areas of study.

Life science

Entomology is one of several sciences that focus on life and how it works. It's a part of zoology, the study of animals – because insects are a type of animal. And zoology is a part of biology, the study of living things, or organisms.

What's in a name?

Why is it called entomology, and not insectology? The name comes from two Greek words, *logy* meaning study, and *entomon*, meaning cut or divided into sections. The ancient Greek scientist Aristotle gave insects this name because of their three separate body parts.

Scientists first used the modern word "entomology" in 1764. In those days it was common to use old Greek words for science names.

INSECT SCIENCE HISTORY

We've been learning about insects for a long time ...

Prehistory

Ancient rock paintings show someone collecting honey.

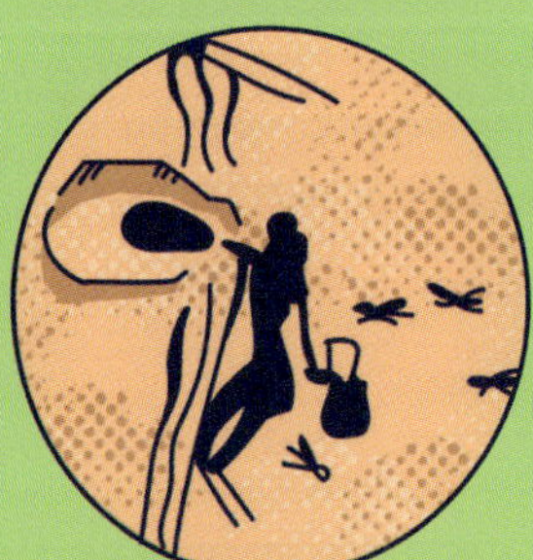

350 BCE

Aristotle wrote about insects in his book *History of Animals*.

Branches and areas

Most entomologists don't study everything about insects, or all the different species. Instead they focus on a special area, or a particular insect type.

For example, you could choose

Myrmecology
the study of ants

Lepidopterology
the study of moths and butterflies

Coleopterology
the study of beetles

Dermapterology
the study of earwigs

That's right – there are scientists who just study earwigs!

Or you could focus on an area such as:

Insect morphology
insects' body shapes and features

Medical entomology
how insects cause or spread diseases

Insect ecology
how insects coexist with other living things in their habitats

Insect taxonomy
sorting insects into different types and groups

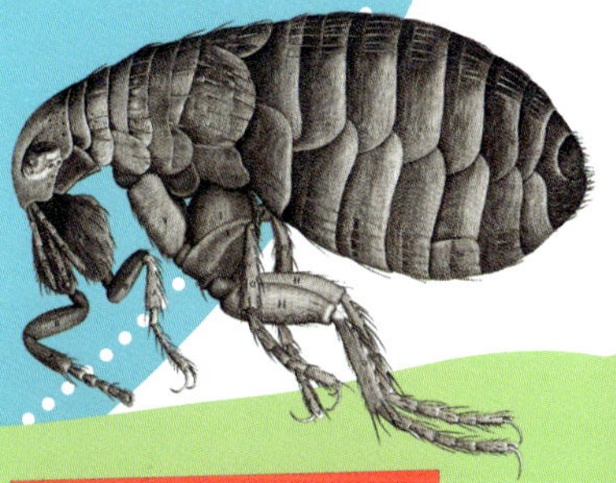

1660s

The invention of microscopes let scientists see insects up close.

1700s

Artist and naturalist Maria Sybilla Merian (see page 20) discovered new insect species in Suriname.

1815–1826

William Kirby and William Spence wrote *An Introduction to Entomology*, a huge insect encyclopedia, paving the way for the modern science of entomology.

THE WORLD OF INSECTS

Insects all have the same basic body parts, but they come in a huge range of shapes and sizes, and are found in all kinds of places all around the world.

Meet the family!

Entomologists sort out insect species, or classify them, into different types and groups. This insect family tree shows you the main groups. Groups that are closer together in the tree are more closely related in real life. For example, stick insects are closely related to grasshoppers, but very different from bees.

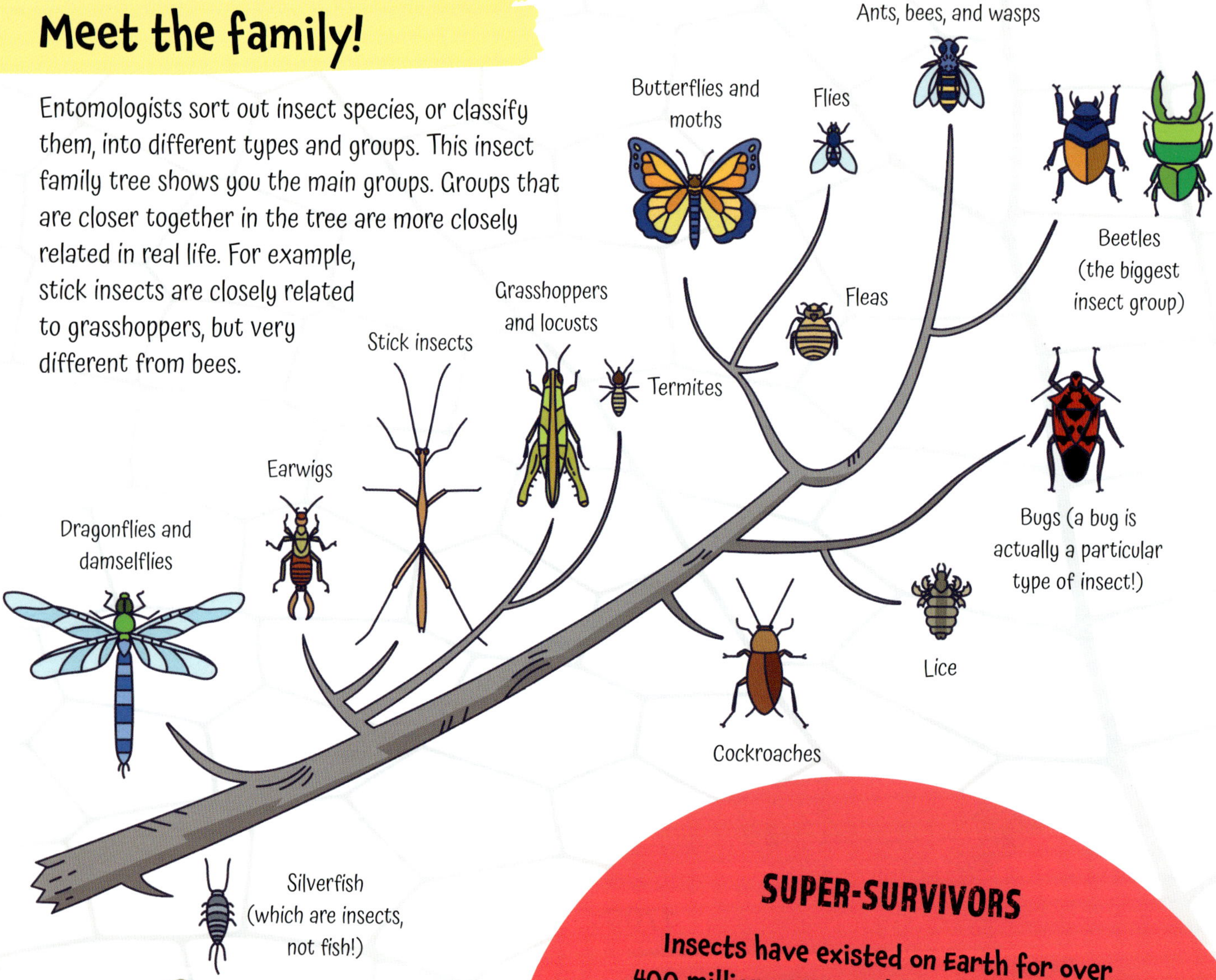

Scientists called paleoentomologists study insect fossils and prehistoric insect life.

SUPER-SURVIVORS

Insects have existed on Earth for over 400 million years, and survived when many other types of animals died out. They were among the first animals to walk on land, and the first to fly in the air. And in prehistoric times, some insects used to be much bigger than they are now. One, called *Meganeura*, looked like a dragonfly and had a 28-inch (70-cm) wingspan!

Where in the world?

Insects live almost everywhere on Earth, in every kind of habitat: forests, meadows, mountains, deserts, caves, swamps, rivers, cities, and inside our homes. Different species have evolved and adapted, or gradually changed over time, to survive in all these different places.

The only places you won't find many insects are the frozen ice sheets of Greenland and Antarctica, and in the sea. Some insects live on beaches, and a few species skate on the sea surface, but insects are not found in the deep oceans. (Scientists are not really sure why.)

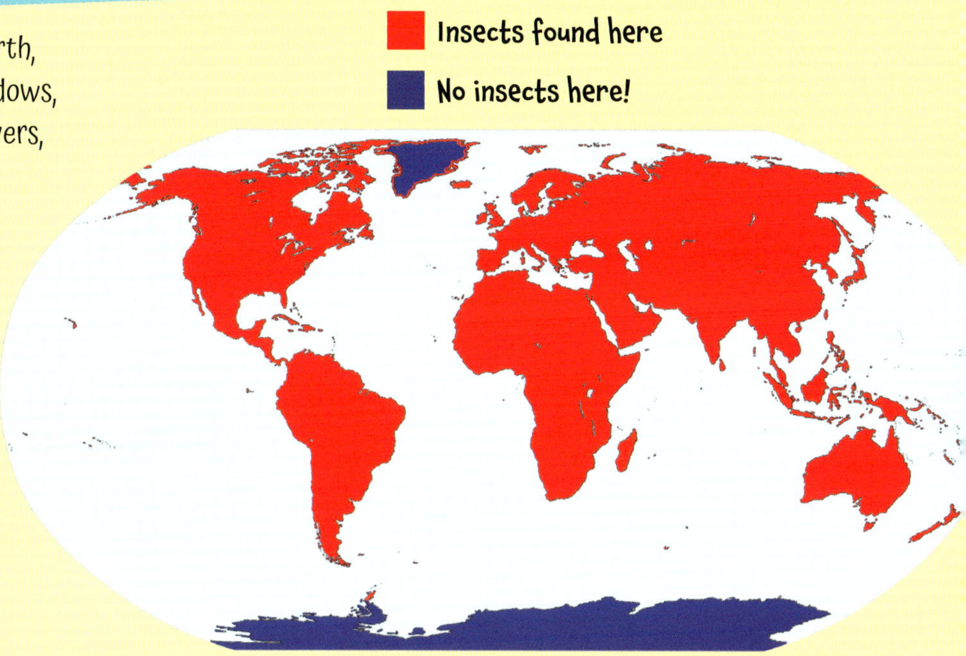

Entomologists visit wild and remote places in search of insects, such as going to Antarctica to study the tiny Antarctic midge along the rocky coastline.

WORKING WITH INSECTS

As an entomologist, you have to work closely with insects. What's it like, and what exactly do entomologists do all day?

It's a mix!

A typical entomologist does a mixture of different kinds of work in their job. These could include:

• Field work

This means working outdoors, though not always in a field! It could be a forest, garden, mountain, or anywhere insects live. You might watch insects to see how they behave, count them to see if a species is endangered, or collect insects to study in the lab.

• Working with collections

Universities and museums often have collections of preserved insects. You might use these for studying, or work as a curator, looking after a collection.

• Computer work

As an entomologist, you would use computers to make scans or simulations of insects, or to write books or papers about your discoveries.

• Lab work

Entomologists also work in science labs, using microscopes to look closely at insects, or to carry out tests on them (such as seeing if ants can solve a maze).

• Teaching

Entomologists in universities teach students and give lectures, as well as doing their own research.

• Sharing the science

You might also write books, visit schools or help to make TV shows, to help the public learn more about insects.

Bug businesses

Entomologists often work for businesses too. That's because insects are so important in areas like health and farming. For example, you could work for a company developing new nets to stop mosquitoes from spreading diseases, or a company that helps beekeepers to keep their bees healthy.

Bees make money for businesses, both by making honey and by pollinating crops.

IS IT DANGEROUS?

It can be! Entomologists have to be careful, as they could get stung or bitten by an insect, infected with a disease, or lost in a wild, remote location.

DO ENTOMOLOGISTS KILL INSECTS?

Yes, this can sometimes happen. Long ago, naturalists often collected insects from the wild, killed them, and preserved them. Many of those insects are still stored in collections today.

If possible, entomologists study these already-dead specimens instead of catching new ones. But sometimes, they do still kill insects in order to study things like how they carry diseases. However, they must take care not to harm protected endangered species, and to treat insects with as much respect as possible.

The famous fruit fly

Case Study

Have you ever seen tiny little flies hovering around a compost bin or a fruit bowl? These are fruit flies, and they're not just nuisance fruit-raiders. They're insect science stars!

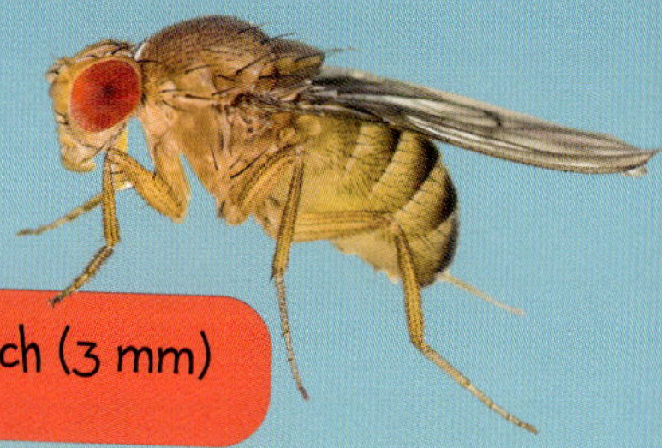

Why this fly?

Scientists have been studying fruit flies for over 100 years. They are very good insects for studying in a lab, because ...

- They breed very quickly, growing from egg to adult in about 2 weeks
- They have lots of babies at once – a female lays around 40 eggs per day
- They're small and easy to feed, so it's easy to keep lots of them in the lab.

Thomas Hunt Morgan set up the famous "Fly Room" at Columbia University in New York, where he and his students could breed and study millions of fruit flies.

Flies and genes

In the early 1900s, American biologist Thomas Hunt Morgan used fruit flies to study how living things pass on their features to their babies in their genes – the tiny parts inside cells that control how they work. Fruit flies have been used ever since to find out more about genes and DNA.

To breed fruit flies in the lab, scientists keep them in jars or tanks and feed them sugar and yeast.

Fruit fly discoveries

Besides genes and DNA, fruit flies are used to study many other things, such as ...

- How insect life cycles work
- How animal cells work
- How viruses attack cells, including the COVID-19 virus
- How to stop flies and other pests from ruining fruit crops
- How pollution affects cells and genes
- How insects age and get old.

Like many other insects, fruit flies go through metamorphosis, changing from a worm-like larva (baby) into an adult with legs and wings (see page 22).

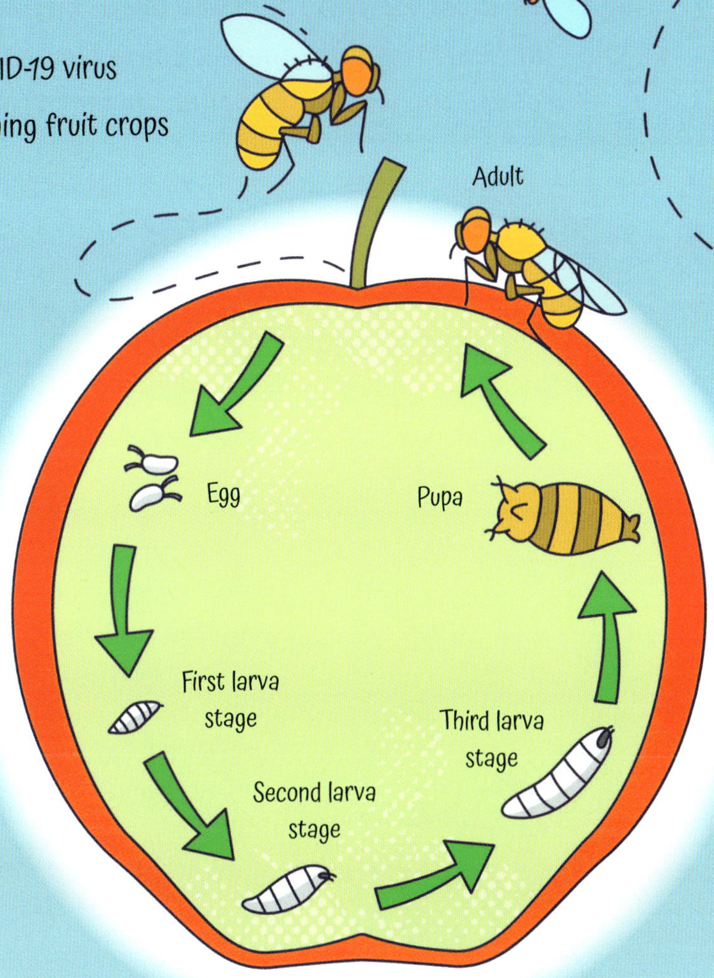

Flies in space!

Fruit flies have even been sent into space to find out how microgravity affects their cells and life cycle. In fact, they were the first animals to be sent to space in 1947.

FACT FILE

FRUIT FLY

NAME: *DROSOPHILA MELANOGASTER*

INSECT GROUP: DIPTERA (FLIES)

FIRST DESCRIBED AND NAMED: 1830

SIZE: 0.07-0.1 INCH (2-3 MM) LONG

IN THE FIELD

One of the most exciting parts of being an entomologist is going on field trips. This means going outdoors to watch insects in the wild, or to collect insects to study.

Catching and collecting

Most insects are small, and many of them can fly. This can make it hard to keep track of what they're doing. So collecting insects is a big part of field trips, either to study them in the field, or to take them back to the lab. To catch them, entomologists use a range of traps and other devices:

• Nets

Insect collectors in cartoons use nets, but they're very useful in real life too.

- A sweep net for catching flying insects
- A water net for water insects

• Light trap

A light trap like this can collect moths and other night-flying insects.

• Pitfall trap

A container in the ground for catching ground-dwelling bugs

• Malaise trap

This is a tent-like trap made of netting, for catching insects as they fly along it.

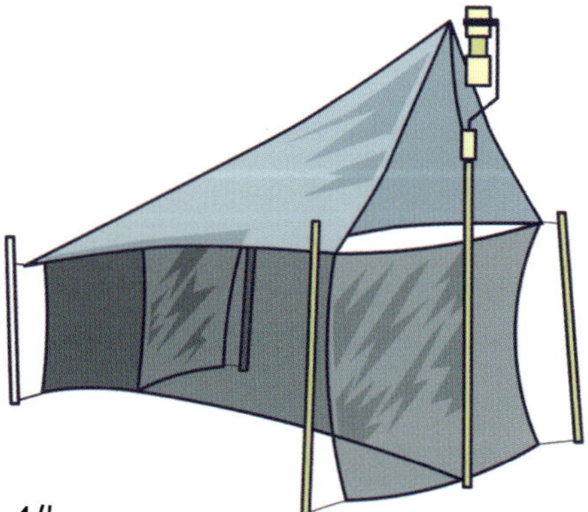

• Suction trap

This is a bit like a leaf blower in reverse. It sucks insects up into a container.

• Beating tray

A large square of cloth stretched out on a frame, which you hold below a bush or tree branch. Then you shake or hit the branch, and insects fall out onto the tray.

THE POOTER

The pooter is a handy mini device for picking up small insects. It's named after its inventor, U.S. entomologist William Poos!

These entomologists are collecting insects in the canopy, or upper level, of a eucalyptus forest in Australia, using a platform suspended between the trees to work on.

Watching and observing

Sometimes, instead of collecting insects, you just watch them, count them or look for signs of them, such as their eggs, damage to plants, or even the sounds they make. To look at them closely, entomologists use magnifying glasses, or take photos or videos.

OUTDOOR SKILLS

To find the insects you're interested in, you might have to trek somewhere remote, camp in the wilderness, or even go climbing, diving, or caving. Entomologists take classes to learn the special skills they need.

IN THE LAB

Back in the lab, entomologists use scientific equipment to take a closer look at insects and conduct experiments with them.

Under the microscope

The microscope is one of the most important lab tools, as seeing insects in close-up can reveal much more about them. Sometimes entomologists study dead insects this way, for example to look at their body parts or insides, but they look at living insects too.

This is an optical or light microscope, which uses lenses to magnify the insects.

A microscope reveals that the colors on a butterfly's wings are made up of tiny scales arranged in patterns.

Insect experiments

To study how living insects breed and grow, behave, move, or sense things, entomologists keep them in the lab in tanks or jars. Sometimes they use equipment that can hold on to an insect without harming it. For example, a flight mill attaches to an insect while it's flying, so that it moves around in a circle. It can measure the insect's speed and how far it has flown. You can also video the flight to watch it in slow motion.

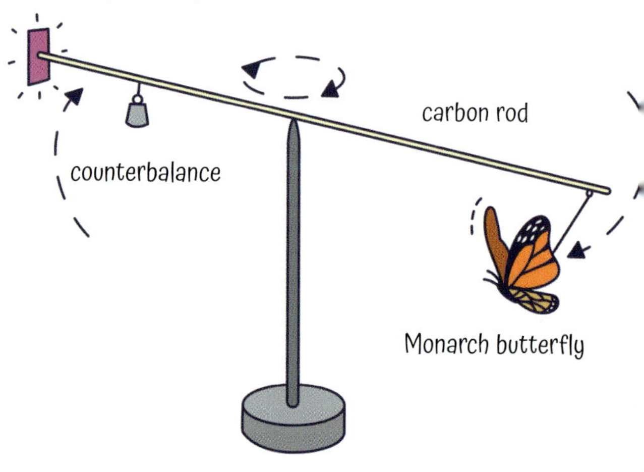

Ant mazes

Mazes can be used to test insect intelligence, memory, and communication. Here's one example of a type of maze that's often used to test ants, called a Y maze.

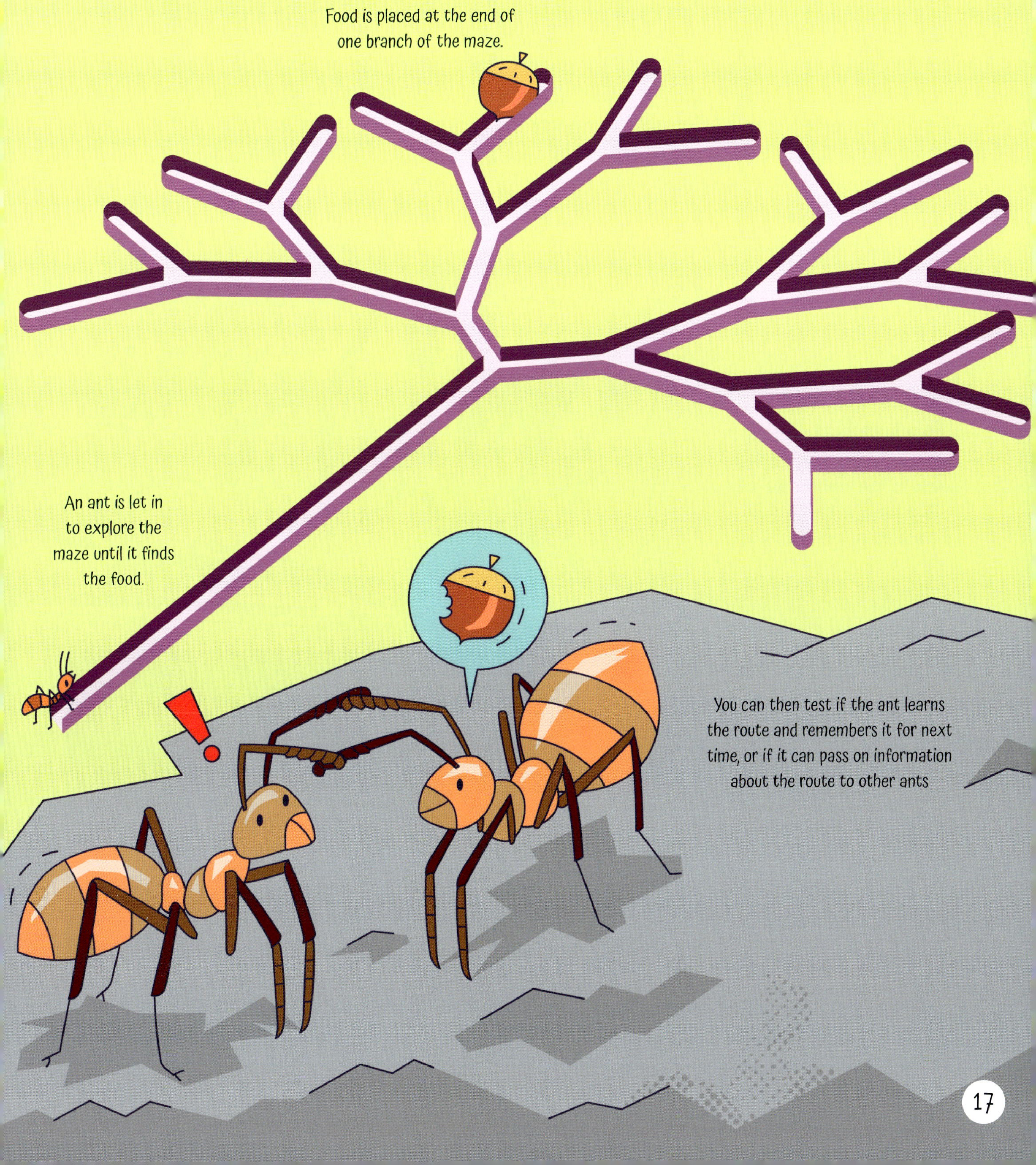

NEW DISCOVERIES

Entomologists have discovered and named around a million insect species, but they think there could be millions more out there waiting to be discovered ...

Finding new species

Every year, scientists discover thousands of new insect species. Often, they're found in wild, unexplored places, like high mountaintops, wild jungles, or remote islands, but not always. They can turn up anywhere, even in busy cities.

This huge and beautiful new butterfly species was found in the remote Natewa Peninsula in the Pacific island nation of Fiji in 2018.

From old to new

Sometimes, entomologists know about a type of insect, but they think it belongs to an existing species - until new information shows it's actually a different species. That's what happened with this stunning stick insect from Madagascar in Africa. A study of its genes and DNA showed that it was a separate species, and it got its own name, *Achrioptera maroloko*, in 2019.

Most stick insects are green or brown and perfectly camouflaged as sticks. This species is unusual because the males are brightly colored – to attract a mate, or to warn predators that they taste bad, or maybe both.

New names

When entomologists find a new species, they get to name it. All species of living things have their own unique scientific name so that scientists around the world always know which is which, whatever language they speak.

Papilio natewa

"Papilio" means butterfly.

★ **A species name has two parts, and is always written in *italics*.**

★ **The name often describes something about the species.**

"natewa" is the name of the area the butterfly comes from.

BUGS WITH GEARS

Sometimes, entomologists make amazing new discoveries about common insects. For example, this planthopper bug was first studied and named in 1781. But in 2013, scientists discovered how the young bug has two tiny gears on its legs that lock together when it hops. It's the first animal ever found to have working gears.

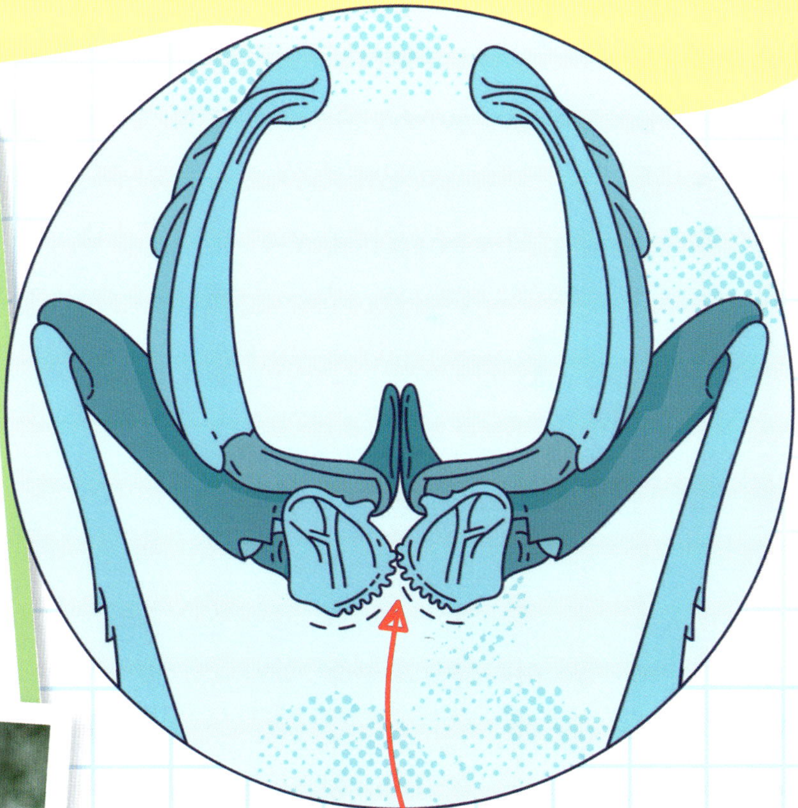

The gears lock together to make sure the bug's legs both push off at the same time.

Case Study

Maria Sibylla Merian

In the 1600s, many people believed that creepy-crawlies like insects and worms grew from nothing, appearing like magic in mud or rotting food. The Swiss naturalist and insect artist Maria Sybilla Merian helped to change this with her studies of insect life cycles.

The art of nature

Maria Sybilla Merian was born in 1647. After her father died when she was three, her mother married a famous flower artist, Jacob Marrel. Maria learned to paint in his studio, and by the age of 13 she was creating her own nature artworks.

Maria was also fascinated by caterpillars. She collected and bred them, sketched them and made notes about how they changed into butterflies and moths.

Caterpillar crazy!

When she grew up, Merian became a drawing teacher and flower artist. But her passion was still caterpillars! She kept studying and painting them, and in 1679, she published a book on them, called *Der Raupen wunderbare Verwandlung und sonderbare Blumennahrung* – "The wonderful transformation of caterpillars and their strange floral diet."

Maria described her work in one of her books:

"I spent my time investigating insects. At the beginning, I started with silk worms in my home town of Frankfurt. I realized that other caterpillars produced beautiful butterflies or moths, and that silkworms did the same. This led me to collect all the caterpillars I could find in order to see how they changed."

Merian collected European silkmoth caterpillars like these.

Insect mysteries

Merian's work on caterpillars was not just beautiful art, but important science. Around this time, scientists were doing experiments to try to find out how insects were born. Did they really grow from mud or food – known as "spontaneous generation"? Or were they born from parents, like other animals?

Merian helped to answer this by revealing insect life cycles: butterflies and moths laying eggs, eggs hatching, and caterpillars transforming into adults. She painted living insects, not just dead specimens, allowing her to see how they changed through their lives.

Merian's illustration of the white witch moth and its cocoon and caterpillar, from her 1705 book *Metamorphosis of the Insects of Suriname*

A trip to the tropics

Later, from 1699 to 1701, Merian and her daughter Dorothea went on a journey to Suriname in South America, to study the insects in its tropical jungles. She published a second caterpillar book in 1705, full of paintings of them, including species previously unknown to science.

FACT FILE

MARIA SYBILLA MERIAN

BORN: 1647, FRANKFURT, GERMANY

NATIONALITY: SWISS

DIED: 1717, AMSTERDAM, NETHERLANDS

INSECT LIFE CYCLES

Like Maria Sybilla Merian, entomologists today still breed insects in captivity to study their life cycles, and how they reproduce, or have babies.

Metamorphosis

Metamorphosis is the way some insects change during their life cycle, such as a caterpillar changing into a butterfly. To do this, the larva, or baby insect, becomes a pupa or chrysalis.

Inside the pupa, most of the larva's body breaks down into a slimy liquid. The ingredients rebuild themselves to make the parts of the adult insect.

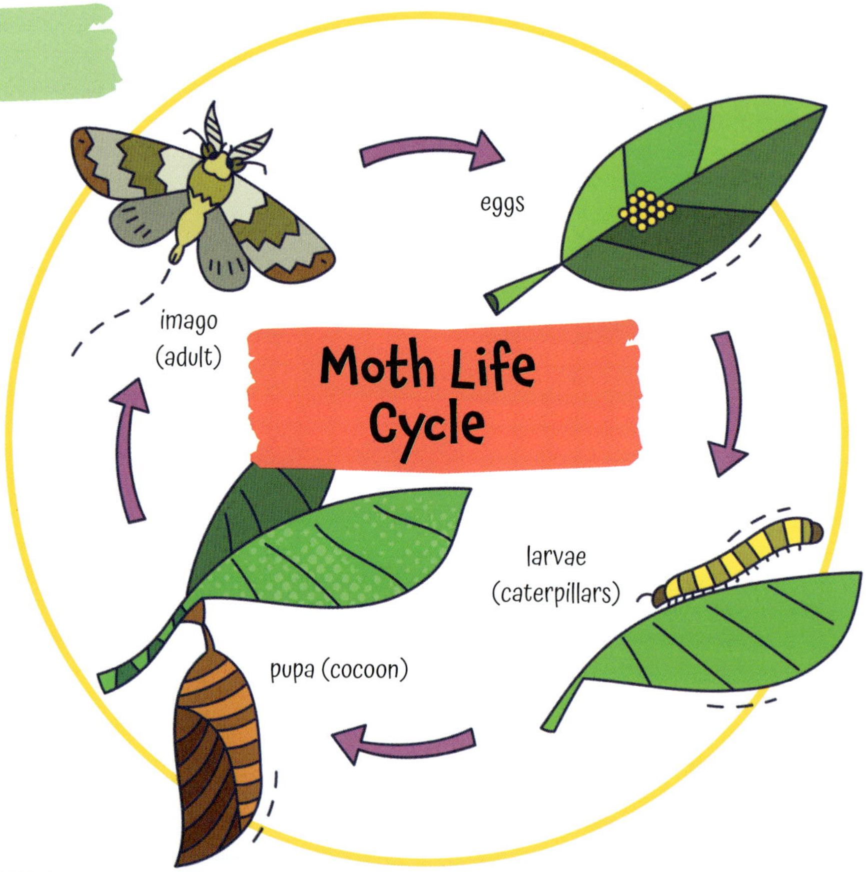

Mini me

Some insects don't change this much. Instead, like humans, their babies look like tiny versions of the adults and gradually grow bigger.

Aphids, a type of small plant-eating bug, give birth to tiny live babies, called nymphs.

Finding a host

Quite a few insect species lay their eggs in another living thing so that the baby has food to eat when it hatches. That could be a fruit, a flower, or even another animal!

A female tarantula hawk wasp fights and stings a tarantula to paralyze it, then drags it into her burrow. She lays an egg on it, then when the baby hatches, it feeds on the tarantula.

Water-dwellers

Mosquitoes, midges, mayflies, caddisflies, and many more insects lay their eggs in water. The larvae live underwater until they are ready to become flying adults.

A caddisfly larva builds itself a protective case from pebbles or sand.

Baby care

Most insects leave their eggs to hatch, and the larvae have to find their own food. But some, such as bees, ants, and earwigs, look after and feed their babies.

A female earwig with her eggs and babies. She moves the eggs around using her jaws, and nibbles dirt off them to keep them clean.

SOLVING CRIMES

Forensic entomologists use expert knowledge about insect life cycles to help solve crimes, especially murders. But how?

- When someone dies, insects such as blowflies arrive to lay their eggs on the body.
- If you know exactly how long each stage of a fly's life cycle takes, you can use eggs or larva found on the body to calculate exactly when the person died. This can be vital evidence in a murder case.

INSECT BEHAVIOR

Why do insects do what they do? Are they smart and can they learn? Entomologists studying insect behavior ask questions like these, and observe or test insects to find out the answers.

Insects do many amazing things, like this praying mantis dancing to attract a female.

Is it instinct?

Instinct means automatic behavior that an animal doesn't have to learn. Entomologists often call it "innate" behavior, meaning it's built into the insect's brain. But not all behavior is innate, even in insects.

For example, honeybees instinctively know how to fly, suck nectar from flowers, and build their honeycomb with hexagon-shaped cells.

But honeybees are not born knowing what kinds of flowers grow near their hive or nest. Over time, they learn which colors and shapes of flowers have the most nectar, and learn where they are so that they can fly straight to them.

Insect intelligence tests

How do you test an insect's intelligence and learning skills? Entomologists have come up with some brilliant experiments, such as this string-pulling test for bumblebees.

Scientists put artificial flowers containing food, attached to strings, under a clear piece of plastic. Bumblebees can only get the food if they pull a string to move the flower nearer.

At first, only two bumblebees, out of a group of 110, figured it out. But after watching other bees do it, most bumblebees could learn how to get the food.

This shows that a few bumblebees are smart – but even those who aren't can learn new tricks.

Observing antlions

It can be difficult to study insect behavior in the wild, as insects often don't stay where you want them. So entomologists sometimes recreate an insect's habitat in the lab. There, they can watch the behavior carefully, and make videos and measurements.

Antlions are the larvae of a group of insects called lacewings. They dig cone-shaped pits in sand and hide at the bottom, waiting for ants to fall in and slide down into their large jaws.

WHO'S THE SMARTEST?

According to entomologists, the cleverest insects are:

1 Bees 2 Ants 3 Cockroaches

To study antlion behavior, entomologists collect them, along with the sand they live in and the ants they hunt, and put them in trays in the lab. There, the antlions dig their pits and hunt as normal.

INSECT SOCIETIES

Honeybees don't live alone – instead they live together in a big group, or colony, in a hive or nest. Insects that do this are called social insects.

Living together

Social insects include ants, termites, and some species of bees and wasps. In a colony, different individuals do different jobs to help keep the colony alive and healthy.

Termites live in nests or mounds with lots of tunnels and rooms, or chambers. Here, the huge, sausage-shaped queen is in her royal chamber, being cared for and fed by workers. They also collect her eggs and take them to a nursery chamber to be looked after.

There are several different types of termites in a colony:

Soldier termites guard the nest and attack predators.

Only the queen lays eggs.

The king mates with the queen.

Workers do most of the jobs, like collecting food, building the nest and caring for babies and the queen.

Winged termites fly out of the nest and start new colonies.

Teamwork!

Because they work as a team, social insects can do all kinds of things that one insect could not do on its own. Termites build huge mounds as high as a house from soil, saliva, and their own poop. Army ants make living bridges from their own bodies to get across gaps. A swarm of bees or wasps can scare away a big predator, such as a bear.

A "living bridge" of army ants

Studying social insects

Studying social insects can be tricky, because you're looking at lots of insects at once, and trying to figure out what they're all doing and how they communicate.

In the 1940s, Austrian scientist Karl von Frisch discovered how honeybees do dances to tell each other where they've found food. To watch them, he used observation hives with glass windows, and painted dots on individual bees so he could follow their movements. Entomologists still use these methods today.

DID YOU KNOW?

Some entomologists say that a social insect colony exists and "thinks" more like a single living thing than a group of individuals. They call this a "superorganism."

Radar routes

To see where bees go when they fly out of their hive or nest, entomologists use radar.

They attach tiny trackers to the bees, like this, and pick up signals from them as the bees fly around.

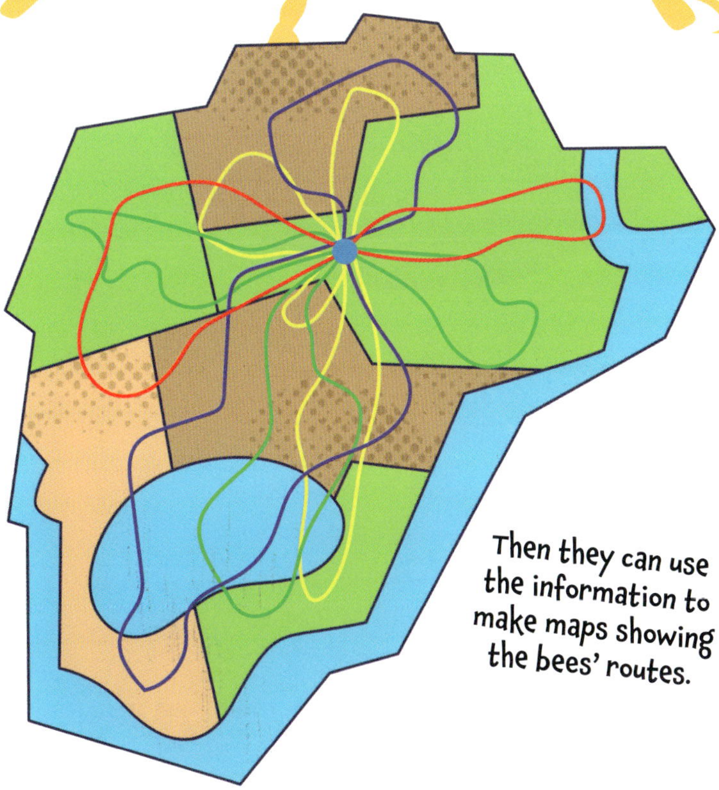

Then they can use the information to make maps showing the bees' routes.

Case Study

The Asian giant hornet

The hornet you can see here is shown at actual size! It's an Asian giant hornet, the biggest hornet species in the world, with a body up to 2 inches (5 cm) long.

What is a hornet?

Hornets are a type of large wasp. Like common wasps, they live in a colony, and build a papery nest out of chewed wood. There are several different hornet species.

A colony of Asian giant hornets is smaller than a typical wasp colony, with only a few hundred hornets.

FACT FILE

ASIAN GIANT HORNET

NAME: *VESPA MANDARINIA*

INSECT GROUP: HYMENOPTERA (WASPS, BEES AND ANTS)

FIRST DESCRIBED AND NAMED: 1852

SIZE: 1.5-2 INCHES (4-5 CM) LONG

Asian giant hornets are native to Japan, but also live in other parts of Asia.

Hornets in the news

Asian giant hornets are fascinating insects in themselves. But recently, entomologists have been studying them more than ever. That's because they are spreading outside their normal range, or home area, to new countries.

Since 2019, they've also been found in the western United States and Canada.

What's the problem?

It's not always a problem when a species spreads to a new area, but it can be. If it harms the ecosystem (see page 32) in its new home, it's called an invasive species. Asian giant hornets are an invasive species in North America, because they are a danger to local honeybees. Working as a group, they raid a hive or nest, kill the bees and steal the larvae and pupae to feed to their own babies.

On the case

Because of this, entomologists are working hard to find invasive giant hornets and collect them. One method is to attach a tiny radar tag to any hornets that are found, then track them back to their nests to find the others.

BEE BALL

In Japan, honeybees have evolved a way to fight back against Asian giant hornet attacks. They surround each hornet in a group of bees, called a "bee ball," and vibrate their muscles to create heat, which kills the hornet. But as North American bees don't do this, they're in more danger.

USEFUL INSECTS

Humans use insects to help us, especially a few key species. They provide us with valuable products, pollinate our crops, and can even be used as food.

• Silk moth

Silk is made from the threads that silk moth caterpillars spin to make their cocoons.

• Blowfly

The maggots (or larvae) of blowflies are important in forensic science (see page 23) and are also used in hospitals to clean infected wounds.

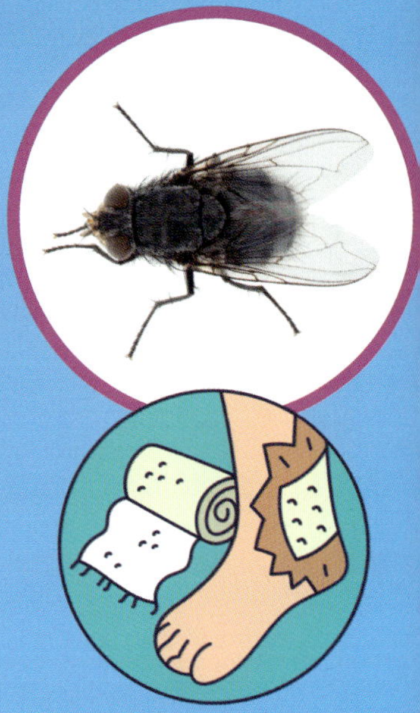

• Mopane moth

The caterpillars of mopane moths, known as mopane worms, are an important food in southern Africa.

• Cochineal bug

Cochineal bugs are ground up to make red dyes called carmine, used in make-up and food coloring.

• Honeybee

Honeybees help farmers all over the world by pollinating fruit trees and other crops.

They also make honey and beeswax.

Studying the science

It's important for entomologists to study these useful insects, to find out more about them, and find solutions when things go wrong. They work on things like:

• Insect diseases

Some entomologists study the diseases and pests that affect insects including honeybees and silkworms, and look for ways to treat or cure them.

• Finding alternatives

Others study insect products like silk and carmine dye, and work on other ways of making them, instead of using insects.

• Insect farming

Insect farming is increasing around the world, as a way to grow more food in less space. Entomologists help insect farmers find the best ways to breed insects and treat them humanely.

IS IT WRONG TO USE INSECTS?

Should we really be using insects to make things for us, or killing and eating them?

We use many other kinds of animals for food, for wool, or for riding and carrying loads.

Some people argue that insects actually suffer less than other farm animals, as they don't live long and don't need much space.

But others, such as vegans, disagree with using any kind of animal for our own needs.

What do you think?

NEW USES

Entomologists also work on new ways we can make use of insects, such as:

- Using insects as food for farm animals
- Using bee and ant venom to treat arthritis
- Training bees to sniff out land mines with their antennae, so these can be safely removed.

INSECTS AND ECOSYSTEMS

An ecosystem means a habitat, or surroundings, and the living things that are found in it. In most ecosystems, there are a LOT of insects.

How it works

The species in an ecosystem interact with each other, and feed on each other to survive. Scientists show this as a pyramid made up of several layers or levels.

Tertiary consumers eat other consumers.

Secondary consumers eat primary consumers.

Primary consumers eat plants.

Plants, or producers, are very important too. They use energy from sunlight to grow, providing food for animals.

Decomposers feed on dead plants and animals or waste such as poop. They break down useful chemicals and return them to the soil.

Bats fly out in the evening to feed on millions of moths, midges, and other insects.

Insects feed on plants, pollinating them as they go and helping the plants to make seeds. That makes more plants, providing more food for the ecosystem.

Dung beetles are important decomposers. They roll away animal dung, bury it, and lay their eggs in it.

Insect ecology

An ecosystem works as a whole, with all the species in it existing in a balance. As there are so many insects all over the world, they are a vital part of most ecosystems.

Studying insects and their ecosystems is called insect ecology. As well as finding out how insects affect ecosystems, insect ecologists do a lot of survey work to check on the insects in a habitat. They monitor insect numbers and biodiversity – how many different species there are in a habitat. They also study how things like deforestation, pollution, or climate change affect the ecosystem.

This team of entomologists is carrying out an insect biodiversity survey in Borneo.

EVOLVING TOGETHER

Entomologists also study how some insects live in symbiosis with other species in their ecosystem. This means the two species help each other to survive.

Acacia ants live in symbiosis with the bullhorn acacia tree. The ants live inside the tree's huge thorns and eat food the tree makes for them. In return, they use their stings to guard the tree from larger plant-eaters.

INSECTS IN DANGER

There are a lot of insects in the world. But for the past few decades, their numbers have been falling. What's happening to them?

Insects in decline

To find out what's going on, entomologists have been doing insect surveys all around the world, looking at as many insect species as they can. They've found that the world's insect population seems to be dropping by between 1 percent and 2 percent each year, and has been falling since some time in the 1900s.

To get a good picture of insect populations, entomologists have to check them in many different habitats and climates. This scientist is collecting insects in a tropical jungle at night.

What's causing it?

The studies show that there's not just one reason for this fall, but lots of different reasons – although they're mostly caused by humans. The main causes are:

- Habitat loss – natural, wild areas being turned into farmland, towns, and roads
- Pollution – in the air, water, and soil
- Pesticides and weedkillers – used on farms to kill insect pests, and also to kill weeds, which provide food for many insects
- Climate change – global warming makes it harder for some insect species to survive, and they're also harmed by increasing storms, floods, and wildfires.

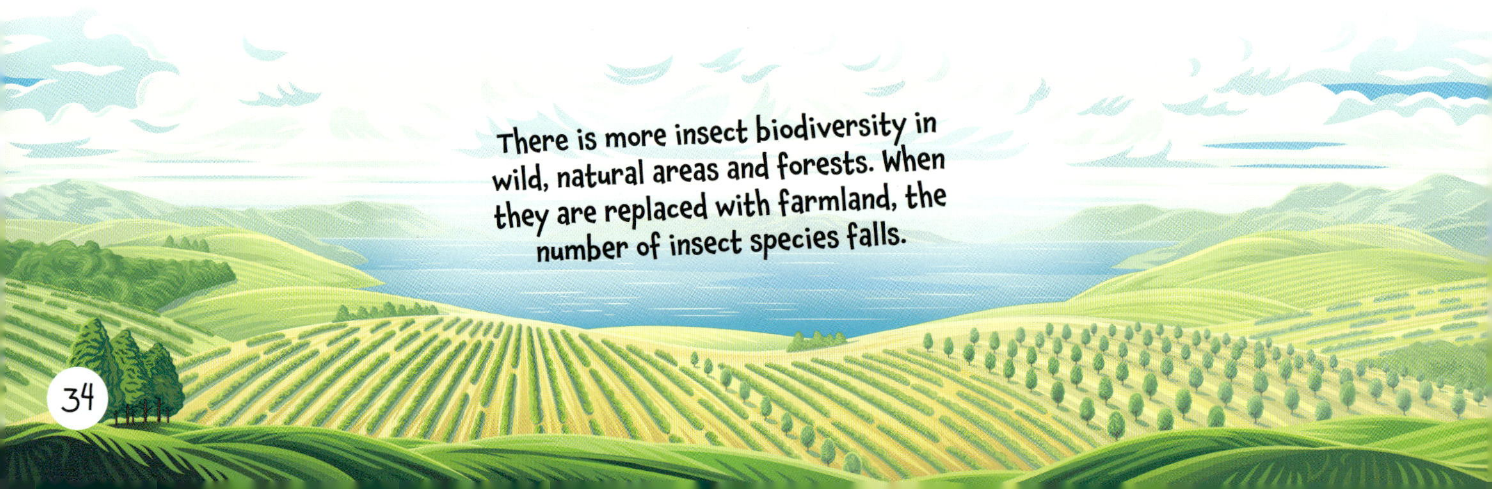

There is more insect biodiversity in wild, natural areas and forests. When they are replaced with farmland, the number of insect species falls.

What can we do?

There are changes we can make to help insects.

- **Setting up wildlife reserves where natural insect habitats are protected**
- **Making laws to ban or reduce pesticides and pollution**
- **Keeping some wild areas on farms and in gardens.**

You can help too, if you have a garden at home or at school. Leaving a corner to grow wild and planting wildflower seeds gives insects food and a place to live.

ENDANGERED SPECIES

Even though they are declining, many insect species are still common. But some are becoming endangered, and at risk of dying out, such as the Queen Alexandra's birdwing butterfly from Papua New Guinea.

NO DECLINE, WE'RE DOING FINE!

Not all insect species are declining. Some, such as household cockroaches, are thriving. They can survive in a range of habitats and eat most foods. And they prefer warmer weather, so global warming is good for them.

Case Study

Goodbye fireflies?

Fireflies are not actually flies, but beetles. They are bioluminescent, meaning they can glow with light, and they use this ability to find a mate.

Bright lights at night

Fireflies are found around the world, in warm, damp forests, meadows, swamps, and riverbanks. On summer evenings, male fireflies fly around flashing their lights on and off, while females sit on the ground or on plants, flashing their lights too. Each species has its own pattern of flashes so that they can find each other.

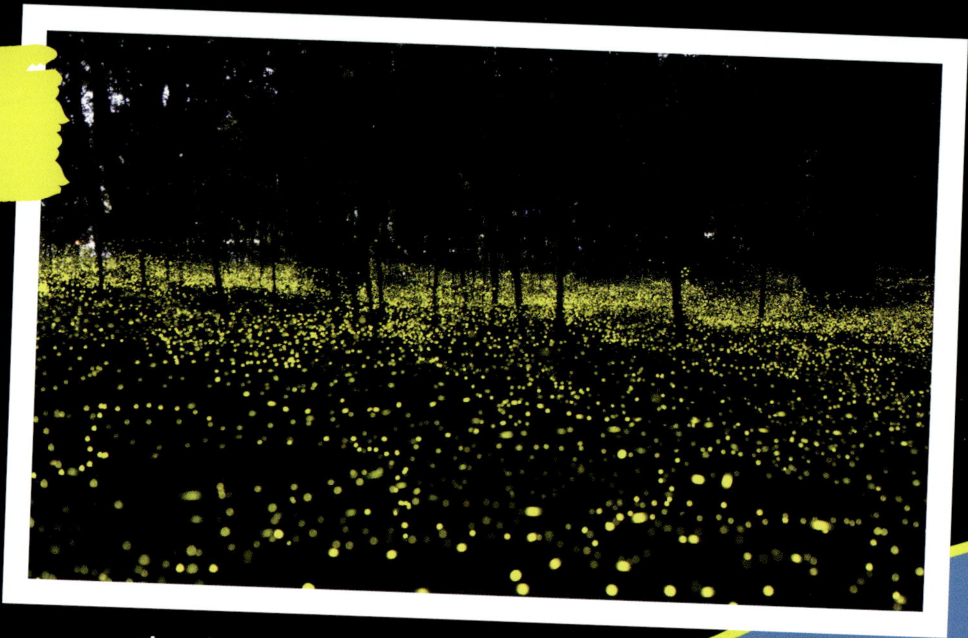

In this photo, thousands of fireflies are lighting up a dark forest in Japan.

Where have they gone?

Many older people remember seeing thousands of fireflies on summer nights, but there are far fewer of them around today. So entomologists have set up studies to see what's happening. They've found that many species of fireflies are less common than they were, and some species are becoming endangered. There are three main reasons:

Pesticides used on farms, and sprayed in swamps to control mosquitoes.

Habitat loss, when forests and swamps are turned into farmland or towns.

And our own bright lights – floodlights, patio lights, security lights, and flashing decorative lights, which confuse the fireflies and make it harder for them to see each other.

Helping fireflies

We can help fireflies to recover, and save them from dying out, in lots of ways:

- **Avoid using pesticides in gardens and on farms**
- **Turn off outdoor lights at night**
- **Close curtains or blinds when lights are on indoors**
- **Keep some area of grass long, to give fireflies hiding places**
- **Set up wildlife reserves in firefly habitats.**

In China, firefly expert Fu Xinhua breeds fireflies to release into the wild and helps people make their villages firefly friendly. This helps the villagers too, as firefly larvae (babies) feed on slugs and snails, which is useful for farmers.

A firefly larva feeding on a slug

Fireflies make their green, yellow, or orange light by combining chemicals in their abdomens that glow as they react together.

FACT FILE

FIREFLIES

INSECT GROUP: *LAMPYRIDAE*

NUMBER OF SPECIES: ABOUT 2,000

FIRST DESCRIBED AND NAMED: 1817

SIZE: 0.15-1 INCH (4-25 MM) LONG

INSECT PESTS

No one wants to find a maggot inside their apple, or cockroaches in their pantry. So what can we do about insect pests?

Munch munch!

There are thousands of insect pest species that love to feed on our crops, stored food, and other things too, such as clothes and carpets. Here are just a few of them ...

Aphids eat crops and garden plants.

Clothes moths lay eggs in natural fabrics, such as wool, and the larvae nibble holes in them.

Weevils feed on crop plants, flour, rice, and other stored food.

Cockroaches like to live in our homes, where they raid food stores and spread germs.

The cotton bollworm is a type of caterpillar that eats cotton plants, and other crops such as beans, peanuts, and tomatoes.

Locusts are grasshoppers that form huge swarms and gobble up whole fields of crops in minutes.

Problems with pesticides

In the 1900s, scientists developed lots of powerful chemical pesticides (meaning "pest killers"). They were very good at killing insect pests, but after a while, we began to realize that pesticides can cause problems. They harm other, helpful insects, such as bees, cause pollution, and damage ecosystems. They're bad for human health too. So we need other ways to stop insects from eating our stuff!

WHAT IS A PEST?

Pests aren't a particular type of insect, just as weeds aren't a particular type of plant. They're just insects that we humans find annoying because they cause problems for us. If we try to kill them all, we also harm ecosystems and Earth as a whole – so it's better to try to find ways to live alongside them.

Pest entomology

Lots of entomologists work in this area. They develop and test ways to control pests without causing more problems. For example, instead of spraying pesticides onto plants, we can use other insects that feed on the pests, natural germs that infect them, or traps that attract them with food, smells, light, or sound.

These mealybugs are ready to be released into a farmer's field, where they will eat bugs called scale insects that damage the crops.

CONFUSED CLOTHES MOTHS

Pheromones are scents that animals use to send messages to each other, and they're sometimes used in insect traps. One new invention, called a moth decoy, uses pheromones to trick clothes moths and stop them from mating and laying eggs.

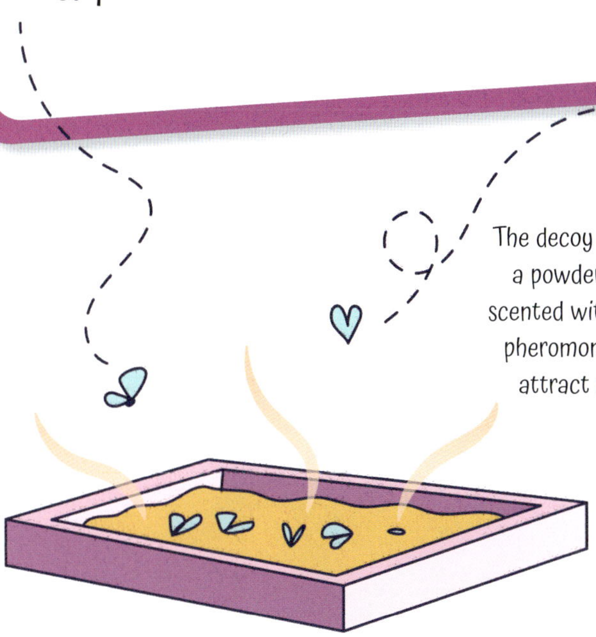

The decoy contains a powdery wax scented with female pheromones that attract males.

When a male arrives, the powder rubs off on him.

He now smells like a female. Other males follow him, but females stay away – so no mating happens!

BITES, STINGS, AND DISEASES

Insects are small, but a lot of people are terrified of them! That's partly because quite a few of them can bite or sting.

Leave us alone!

Biting or stinging makes sense for insects, as it's a good way to fight off bigger predators who want to eat them, or in the case of honeybees, steal their honey. The main stinging insects are bees, wasps, and ants.

Insect stings hurt a lot because as well as sticking into you, the sting injects venom that kills cells.

Munching mandibles

Other insects fight off enemies with a bite from their powerful jaws, called mandibles. Praying mantises, dragonflies and some ants and beetles can bite like this.

Unlike our mouths, an insect's mandibles move sideways, not up and down.

Bite and sting science

Entomologists studying bites and stings have made some amazing discoveries ...

- In Australia, scientist Dr. Ciara Duffy found that a chemical found in bee venom can kill cancer cells. It could be used to make a new cancer treatment.

- Researchers studying trap-jaw ants found that they have the fastest bite in the world – they snap their jaws shut at up to 140 miles (230 km) per hour! They use their bite to catch prey, and also to spring themselves into the air to avoid danger.

Blood suckers

Some insects bite in a different way. Instead of jaws, they have a mouth like a needle, called a proboscis, which jabs into you. They bite people or animals to suck their blood. Mosquitoes, midges, fleas, bed bugs, and kissing bugs are all bloodsuckers.

A mosquito sucking blood

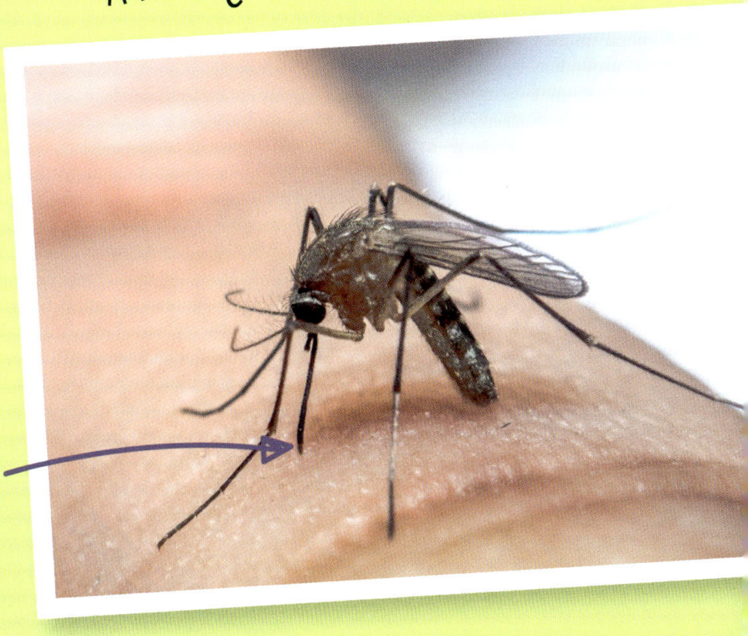

Proboscis

Sometimes this kind of bite just leaves you with a sore or itchy spot. But some bloodsucking bugs can carry germs, which enter your body when they bite you. For example, mosquitoes spread several dangerous diseases, including malaria, yellow fever, and Zika virus.

Can we fix it?

Many people still die each year from diseases spread by insects, but the number is falling as entomologists and other scientists find new treatments and solutions.

A scientist testing blood cells infected with malaria as part of work to develop a malaria vaccine

ENTOMOLOGY TECHNOLOGY

By studying how insects' body parts work, scientists are finding all kinds of new ideas to use in hi-tech inventions and machines.

Inspired by insects

Using living things to inspire inventions is called biomimicry. Check out these brilliant insect biomimicry creations ...

Dragonfly drone

Dragonflies fly very fast and accurately to hunt down other insects in flight, using their four large wings to steer.

This microdrone, a very small flying robot, is designed to fly like a dragonfly. It has four very lightweight wings made from thin sheets of silicon, the material used to make computer chips.

Compound eye camera

Many insects have big round compound eyes, made up of hundreds or thousands of tiny separate lenses. They've inspired a camera lens that works the same way.

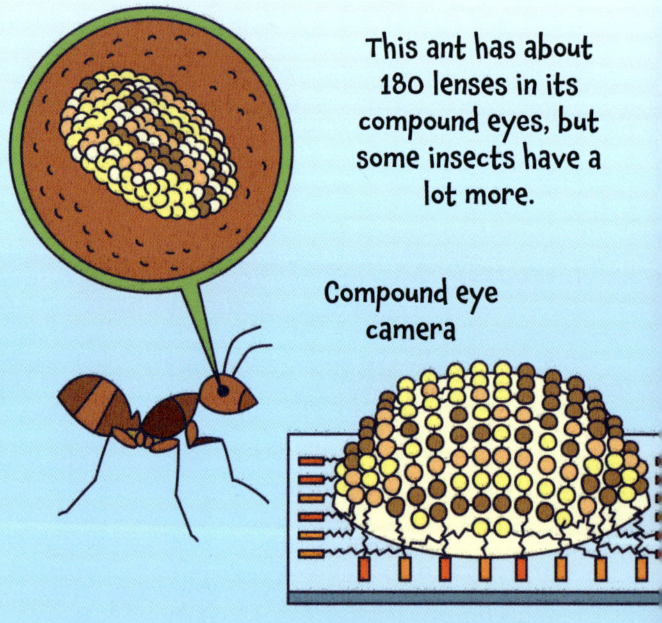

The camera lens has 180 lenses too, and can see in many directions. Scientists are working on making cameras like this with even more lenses. As they're only 0.4 inch (1 cm) across, they could be attached to microdrones to help them detect or photograph things.

Drill like a wasp

Some female wasps have a body part that looks like a huge sting, but is actually an ovipositor, used to lay eggs. It can drill into wood to lay eggs inside trees or logs.

Instead of spinning around like a DIY drill, the ovipositor has three parts that slide against each other, holding the ovipositor still as it bores into the wood.

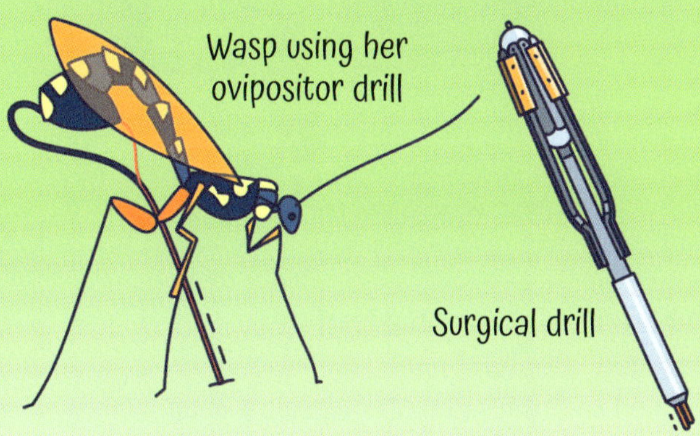

Scientists have copied this to make new tools for doing delicate surgery and for space probes to use to dig into the ground on other planets.

Moth-eye solar panels

Moths' eyes are very non-reflective, so they absorb as much light as possible at night, instead of reflecting it.

This is because moth eyes are covered in microscopic pillars that trap the light. Scientists copied this pattern to make solar panels that soak up as much light as possible too.

WHAT NEXT?

There are probably thousands or even millions of insects that haven't even been discovered yet. They could have amazing abilities and body parts that will inspire the inventions of the future. So we need lots more entomologists to find and study them!

IS ENTOMOLOGY YOUR OLOGY?

Would you love to be an entomologist, exploring the world in search of amazing insects, and finding out all about them? Well, you can!

Insect science skills

What skills and qualities make the best entomologists? It will help if you can check off at least some of these.

• Love insects!

If you run away screaming at the sight of a creepy-crawly, this might not be the life for you! You have to love insects, be fascinated by them, and be OK with being near them and touching them.

• Attention to detail

You'll need to observe insects closely – their behavior, movements, body shapes, colors, and patterns – and set up experiments carefully too.

• Patience

It can take a looooong time to find insects in the wild and see them doing the thing you're interested in, such as a mating dance or hunting behavior.

• Love the outdoors

For entomology fieldwork, you might have to hike, trek, climb, and camp in some wild and remote, hot, cold, or wet places.

• Speaking, writing, and teamwork

Most entomologists have to write about what they've discovered, give talks, and work as a team with other scientists.

SUBJECTS TO STUDY

As you get older, you get to choose your favorite subjects to study. Which ones will help you become an entomologist?

Biology is the most useful – the science of living things.

Math, computer science, and **other sciences** are also a good idea.

Then you can study **biology, zoology,** or **entomology** in college.

What else could you do?

There are lots of other ways to work with insects too. You could be ...

- A roboticist, designing insect-inspired robots
- A doctor or medical scientist working on diseases spread by insects
- A lab technician, breeding and caring for fruit flies or other insects in the lab
- A conservationist, campaigning to protect endangered insect species
- A creative insect photographer, camera operator, or artist
- A science communicator, making TV shows or writing books about insects
- A museum curator, looking after and cataloging a big insect collection
- A farmer growing insects to feed the world
- A zookeeper, looking after the insects in a zoo or butterfly house.

GLOSSARY

Abdomen The third and usually largest of an insect's three body sections.

Adaptation Changing over time to suit the surroundings or conditions.

Antennae The two sensing organs, or feelers, on an insect's head.

Biodiversity The variety of living things in a particular habitat, or in the whole world.

Biology The study of living things.

Bioluminescence The ability of a living thing to glow with light.

Biomimicry The science of using living things to inspire inventions and engineering.

Breed To reproduce or have babies.

Camouflage Body shape, color, or pattern that helps a living thing to hide by matching its surroundings.

Canopy The uppermost layer of a forest or jungle, made up of tree branches and leaves.

Cells The tiny units that living things are made up of.

Chrysalis Another word for the pupa of a moth or butterfly.

Classification The process of sorting living things into a system of types and groups.

Climate change A long-term change in climate and weather patterns.

Cocoon A case some insects spin from thread around the pupa.

Colony A group of animals, such as honeybees, that live together and help each other to survive.

Compound eye A type of animal eye made up of many separate mini-eyes.

Computer simulation A copy of a real-life thing or situation programmed into a computer to help scientists to study it.

DNA (short for deoxyribonucleic acid) A chemical found in cells, used to encode instructions that make the cell work.

Ecology The study of ecosystems and how living things interact with each other.

Ecosystem A habitat and the community of living things that are found there.

Endangered At risk of dying out and becoming extinct, or no longer existing.

Evolution A process of gradual change over multiple generations of living things.

Exoskeleton A stiff protective outer covering or shell, found in animals such as insects and crabs.

Field trip Going to find and study insects or other topics in their natural surroundings.

Food chain A sequence of living things, each feeding on the one before it.

Genes Sequences of chemicals arranged along strands of DNA, which act as coded instructions for cells.

Germs Tiny living things that can cause diseases in other living things.

Global warming A gradual increase in Earth's average temperature over the last two centuries, caused by human activities.

Habitat The natural home or environment of a living thing or species.

Habitat loss The destruction of wild natural habitats.

Host A living thing that is used as a home or food source by a parasite.

Infection What happens when germs get inside the body, or a body part.

Instinct A built-in, automatic pattern of behavior in an animal.

Invasive species A species that can damage an ecosystem when it moves to a new area or habitat.

Lab Short for laboratory, a room or building where scientists do tests or experiments.

Land mine A small explosive device hidden under the ground.

Larva A baby insect.

Lens A clear part that light passes through as it enters an animal's eye.

Life cycle The series of changes a living thing goes through as it is born, grows, becomes an adult, and reproduces, or has babies.

Maggot The name for the larva of some types of insects, especially flies.

Mandibles A name for the biting jaws that some insects have.

Metamorphosis The change of shape that some insect larvae go through to become adults.

Monitoring Keeping track of a wild species and checking on its numbers, health, and movements.

Nectar A sugary liquid made inside flowers to attract insects and other animals to pollinate a plant.

Nymph A baby insect that looks quite similar to its parent.

Ovipositor A long tube-shaped part that some female insects have for laying eggs.

Parasite A living thing that lives on or inside another living thing and takes food from it.

Pesticide A chemical used to kill unwanted insects on crops or garden plants.

Pollen Yellow powder released from flowers, containing male plant cells that are needed to make seeds.

Pollination Spreading pollen from one plant to another, which helps plants to make their seeds.

Predator An animal that hunts and eats other animals.

Prehistoric From the time before people began to write down historic records.

Prey An animal that is hunted and eaten by another animal.

Proboscis A tube-shaped mouth that some insects have, used for sucking up liquids.

Pupa A stage some insects go through during metamorphosis.

Radar A way of detecting where something is using radio waves.

Reproduction The way species of living things make copies of themselves, for example by having babies or releasing seeds.

Social insects Species of insects, such as ants, that live together in groups and help each other to survive.

Species The scientific name for a particular type of living thing.

Specimen A sample of a type of living thing, usually collected from the wild in order to study it.

Symbiosis Two or more different species living together and helping each other to survive.

Thorax The middle of an insect's three body sections, which has the legs and wings attached to it.

Tracking Following the movements of a wild animal.

Vaccine A medicine that teaches the body how to fight off a particular disease germ.

Virus A type of tiny germ, much smaller than most bacteria, that reproduces by invading the cells of living things.

Wildlife reserve A wild area set aside for wildlife, and protected to stop it from being changed or damaged by humans.

Zoology The study of animals.

Further reading

BOOKS

My Book of Bugs: A Fact-Filled Guide to the Insect World
(DK Publishing, 2025)

One Million Insects
by Isabel Thomas and Lou Baker Smith
(Welbeck Editions, 2022)

WEBSITES

https://www.pestworldforkids.org/
Fun facts, videos, games and activities all about insects and other bugs.

https://www.amentsoc.org/bug-club/
Bug Club for young entomologists, from the Amateur Entomologists' Society.

Note to parents and teachers: every effort has been made by the Publishers to ensure websites are suitable for children, that they are of the highest educational value, and that they contain no inappropriate or offensive material. However, because of the nature of the Internet, it is impossible to guarantee that the contents of these sites will not be altered. We strongly advise that Internet access is supervised by a responsible adult.

INDEX